THE SEVEN JOYS OF Mary

Romanus Cessario, O.P.

MAGNIFICAT

Paris · New York · Madrid · Oxford

Publisher: Pierre-Marie Dumont
Editor: Romain Lizé
Assistant to the Editor: Grégoire Sabatié-Garat
Copy editor: Susan Barnes
Art Direction: Elisabeth Hébert
Iconography: Isabelle Mascaras
Layout: Elise Borel
Production: Thierry Dubus, Sabine Marioni
Concept and Design: MAGNIFICAT (Romain Lizé, Marthe Rollier)

Artwork: *The Seven Joys of the Virgin* (c. 1480), Hans Memling (c. 1430-1494)
oil on wood, 74.4 in. wide x 31.9 in. high (1.89 x 0.81 m.)
Alte Pinakothek, Munich, Germany
© La Collection / Artothek.
ISBN: 978-1-936260-19-5
First edition: March 2011
Printed by Transcontinental, Canada
© MAGNIFICAT USA LLC

CONTENTS

For

✠ *J. Augustine Di Noia, O.P.*
Archbishop

&

Gabriel O'Donnell, O.P.
Priest

Frères aînés en saint Dominique

on the fortieth anniversary of their priestly ordination
4 June 1970

THE SEVEN JOYS OF *Mary*

Illustrations from *The Seven Joys of the Virgin* (c. 1480)
Hans Memling (c. 1430–1494)

Foreword

When John the Baptist in Elizabeth's womb heard Mary's greeting, he danced for joy in his mother's womb, like David dancing before the Ark of the Covenant. Mary's voice and her *Shalom Aleichem* stirred his heart, and he was "filled with the Holy Spirit, even from his mother's womb." Mary is the Cause of our Joy, *Causa nostrae laetitiae*. As Catholics we rejoice to have Mary as our Mother. Jesus gives us His Mother on Calvary with the words: Behold thy Mother. Her tender love for Christ's family is an immense consolation to all. It is amazing to see the various altars at the National Shrine of the Immaculate Conception depicting the various Marian devotions of the people who make up the mosaic of our Church in America. Our love for her is a characteristic of our Catholic faith and our celebration of that love fills us with joy: on the liturgical feasts that mark the mysteries of our faith, the patronal feasts, May crownings, processions, and pilgrimages to Marian shrines like Guadalupe, Fatima, Knock, Lourdes, Chestahova, and Loretto.

In his apostolic letter, *Rosarium Virginis Mariae*, Blessed Pope John Paul II writes, "To meditate upon the joyful mysteries then is to enter into the ultimate causes and the deepest meaning of Christian joy. It is to focus on the realism of the mystery of the Incarnation and on the obscure foreshadowing of the mystery of the saving Passion. Mary leads us to discover the secret of Christian joy, reminding us that Christianity is first and foremost *evangelion*, good news, which has as its heart and its whole content the person of Jesus Christ, the Word made Flesh, the one Savior of the world" (*Rosarium Virginis Mariae*, #20).

Father Romanus Cessario has once again produced a spiritual masterpiece that combines his serious theological insights with the treasures of popular piety. I have found his reflections to be very useful to recapture the tradition of celebrating *Mary's Seven Joys*.

As a Franciscan I wear a Franciscan Crown Rosary on my cincture, which invites us to meditate on the seven joys of Mary. The Franciscan historian Luke Wadding (1588-1657) dates the origins of the Franciscan Crown to the year 1422, when the Blessed Mary was reported to have appeared to a novice and instructed him to recite a rosary of seven decades in honor of her seven joys. According to the legend this friar adorned Mary's statue with a crown of flowers.

There are various mysteries employed in compiling the seven, taken from the traditional joyful and glorious mysteries, and adding the adoration of the Magi from Luke's Gospel. Personally the sixth joy of Mary, one that comes to us from tradition and that I find most engaging, is the appearance of the Risen Christ to Mary on Easter. The Franciscan tradition is that Jesus appeared first of all to Mary. In many countries a procession of the *Encuentro* of the Risen Lord and the *Gloriosa* is celebrated on Easter. We can only imagine Mary's joy as she encounters the Son she laid in the tomb on Good Friday. This is not documented in the Gospel, but comes from the heart of believers. *Potuit, decuit, ergo fecit!*

As Fr. Romanus observes, there are various formulations of the seven joys. The Franciscan Crown includes the Visitation, his list adds the Ascension. The overall message is that Mary's faithful discipleship is punctuated by joy. The one who is full of grace is filled with joy: "My spirit rejoices

in God my Savior" (Luke 1:47).

In the Gospel Jesus gives us the Beatitudes, promises of blessedness, of happiness and joy for those who are poor in spirit, meek, who hunger and thirst for holiness, who are pure of heart. Mary proclaimed that all generations would call her blessed. She is the embodiment of the Beatitudes, of the joy and blessedness of a life given completely to God. Christ is at the center of her existence. It is this relationship that frames the joys we contemplate in this volume.

The Holy Father has urged us to contemplate the Christian mystery as a genuine "training in holiness." Fr. Romanus' reflections on the seven joys are aids to making our Christian communities "genuine schools of prayer." No one has ever devoted himself to the contemplation of the face of Christ as faithfully as Mary. Again in his Apostolic Letter *Rosarium Virginis Mariae*, the Holy Father states that "The eyes of Mary's heart already turned to Him at the Annunciation . . . thereafter Mary's gaze, ever filled with adoration and wonder, would never leave Him" (#10).

For us who aspire to be Jesus' disciples, learning to gaze at Jesus through Mary's eyes and to experience the joy of the mysteries of our faith is an important part of our spiritual life. May these spiritual joys ease our burdens and lighten our heart, and allow us to dance before the Ark of the Covenant.

Seán Cardinal O'Malley, O.F.M. Cap.
Archbishop of Boston

21 January 2011
Feast of Saint Agnes

*I*NTRODUCTION

Gaude, virgo, dico gaudens
De favore tuo audens
Laeto corde tua plaudens
Replico nunc gaudia

Rejoice, O Virgin, rejoice, I say:
I unfold your joys,
daring to do so by your favor,
lauding you with a joyful heart.

he hymn "The Joys of the Blessed Virgin Mary," whose first stanza introduces these meditations, comes from the pen of the Carthusian priest Conrad of Haimbourg (†1360).[1] Just as Catholics ponder the Seven Sorrows of Mary, a devotion that finds liturgical expression in the September feast of Our Lady of Sorrows, so also they have identified for the purposes of meditation Seven Joys of Mary. Enumerating the joys of Mary began during the Middle Ages, a period when the Catholic imagination focused on the mysteries of Mary's life. These joys have been variously specified, and the present volume follows one traditional enumeration: The Annunciation Made to Mary, The Nativity of the Lord, The Adoration of the Magi, The

Risen Christ's Appearance to His Mother, The Ascension of the Lord, The Descent of the Holy Spirit, and The Assumption and Coronation of the Virgin. As will become clear below, each joy that wells up in the heart of Mary points us toward the divine Person of her Son.

On 25 March 1987, Blessed John Paul II gave the Church his own meditations on the place Mary holds in our salvation. Since the Pope took the occasion to restore certain features of Marian spirituality and devotion that for one reason or another had suffered eclipse during the period immediately following the Second Vatican Council (1962–65), his encyclical *Redemptoris Mater*, Mother of the Redeemer, accomplished a great deal to redirect Marian piety. One passage especially rejoiced those who cherish Mary as a living instrument of their spiritual well-being. Bl. John Paul II revitalized the form of Marian consecration preached by a French diocesan priest and Dominican tertiary Louis-Marie Grignion de Montfort (1673–1716). "I would like to recall," the Pope wrote, "among the many witnesses and teachers of this [Marian] spirituality, the figure of St. Louis-Marie Grignion de Montfort, who proposes consecration to Christ through the hands of Mary, as an effective means for Christians to live faithfully their baptismal commitments."[2] Since its discovery and publication in the 1840s, de Montfort's *Traité de la vraie dévotion à la Sainte Vierge* had occupied a central place in Marian piety. Frederick William Faber produced the first English translation in 1863.[3] We grasp something of Bl. John Paul II's enthusiasm for de Montfort's spiritual classic when we discover that the saint himself had titled his little essay "Préparation au règne de Jésus-Christ"—Preparation for the reign of Jesus Christ!

The cardinal rule of Marian spirituality holds that when one speaks about Mary, one speaks about Christ. The Seven Joys of Mary illustrate this central precept of Marian spirituality and its corresponding devotion. Mary rejoices in those things that God accomplishes for the salvation of the world through his Son. Mary always leads us to Christ. The phrase "Ad Jesum per Mariam" conveys succinctly this mystery of salvation that finds its origin in the providence of God. Mary of Nazareth embodies in a human person the fullest expression of this saving providence. So what follows in fact describes the dynamics of our own salvation. We find ourselves absorbed in the mysteries of Christ that the Church identifies as those that bring Mary joy.

In the ordinary working of divine providence, the Catholic needs a personal introduction to Mary. Just as a child who received only a list of the chemical components of milk but never sucked at the mother's breast would suffer privation, so the Catholic who masters only the theological axioms that touch upon Mary but has not learned to love her within a community lacks something essential for living by faith. One may cite numerous historical examples of loving communities, such as the Marian sodalities and confraternities that still flourish within the Church, to support this claim. The Irishman, Frank Duff (1889–1980), who founded the Legion of Mary, summed up the same lesson when he explained, "The Legion is Our Lady's spirit come to life in people."[4] All in all though, the saints provide the best commentary on the place that Mary holds in the Church. Their devout exuberance confirms an adage attributed to St. Bernard of Clairvaux, "De Maria, numquam satis." Of Mary, one can never say enough. Father Peter John Cameron, O.P., published a book that captures the best of what saints and other holy men and women have said about the liturgical feasts of Mary.[5] The book places him in a long tradition of Catholic priests like St. Louis-Marie de Montfort and St. Alphonsus Maria Liguori (1696–1787) who have spared no effort to praise the glories of Mary.

While I was still a seminarian,

Thomas Dominic Rover, O.P., a Dominican priest of extraordinary grace and talent, provided special lessons on the mystery of Mary's maternal mediation. An accomplished playwright and poet, Father Rover served as a father in faith for many persons. Someone like Father Rover requires discovery. So I am grateful to two Dominican brothers, slightly older than I, who pointed him out to me. And it pleases me greatly to offer them, in observance of the fortieth anniversary of their priestly ordinations, this little book on Mary. I honored Father Rover in an earlier volume on the Christian virtuous life, a freely given grace that enables us to share even now in the joys that rejoice the heart of the Blessed Virgin Mary.[6]

Notes

[1] He served as prior of the Charterhouse in Gaming, Austria. The English version was translated by James Monti from the Latin text in Guido Maria Dreves, S.J., ed., *Analecta Hymnica Medii Aevi: III: Konrads von Haimburg und seiner Nachahmer, Alberts von Prag und Ulrichs von Wessobrun: Reimgebete und Leselieder* (Leipzig, Germany, 1888), pp. 34–35.

[2] Encyclical Letter of Pope John Paul II on the Blessed Virgin Mary in the Life of the Pilgrim Church, *Redemptoris Mater*, no. 48.

[3] Louis-Marie Grignion de Montfort, *A Treatise on the True Devotion to the Blessed Virgin Mary*, trans. F. W. Faber (London, 1863).

[4] Frank Duff, address to the New York Senatus of the *Legio Mariae*, in December 1956.

[5] Peter John Cameron, O.P., *Mysteries of the Virgin Mary: Living Our Lady's Graces* (Cincinnati, OH, 2010).

[6] See my *Virtues, or the Examined Life* (New York, 2002).

The Annunciation
Made to Mary

Gaude, virgo, mater Christi
Verbum verbo concepisti
Dum ab angelo audisti
Ave plena gratia

Rejoice, O Virgin, Mother of Christ:
with a word you conceived the Word,
when you heard from the angel,
"Hail, full of grace."

When the Eternal Son became man in the womb of the blessed Virgin Mary, God fully revealed his plan of salvation to the Church. On March 25, the Church then celebrates a crucial moment in the history of the world: "In the sixth month, the angel Gabriel was sent from God to a town of

Galilee called Nazareth, to a virgin betrothed to a man named Joseph, of the house of David, and the virgin's name was Mary" (Lk 1:26–27). Bl. John Paul II described this moment as follows: "In the salvific design of the blessed Trinity, the mystery of the Incarnation constitutes the *superabundant* fulfillment of the promise made by God to us after original sin."[1] The angel Gabriel tells the blessed Virgin Mary that the Son conceived in her by the power of the Holy Spirit embodies this fulfillment. "And you shall name him Jesus" (Lk 1:31).

In the Hans Memling (c. 1430–1494) painting that depicts the Seven Joys of the Virgin, one sees the Holy Spirit hover over Mary in the form of a dove. This first joy of Mary establishes her as the chosen instrument of the divine superabundance. For divine graces come only from the inexhaustible bounty of God. The first joy of Mary also sets the paradigm for the other six. Mary's joys become our joys. For as St. Joseph learned in his dream, "you are to name him Jesus, because he will save his people from their sins" (Mt 1:21).

Given the time of Easter in the liturgical year, the Church ordinarily celebrates the springtime feast of the Annunciation in proximity to Good Friday. Most years, the feast falls before Holy Week. When 25 March falls within Holy Week, the Annunciation is transferred to a date after Easter. In any event, the two liturgical observances form a certain unity: On the Annunciation, we celebrate the mystery of the Incarnation at the very beginning of its realization on earth, while on Good Friday, we venerate this same mystery at the very end of its realization on earth. Is it not something of a liturgical oddity that Good Friday should fall so close to the Annunciation? St. Thomas Aquinas, "the greatest theologian of the West," would not think so.[2] Why? Aquinas teaches that the Scriptures suggest no other motive for the Incarnation than the forgiveness of our sins.

Good Friday observes the day when Christ merits this forgiveness. Some Christian artists —for example, the fifteenth-century Flemish painter Robert Campin (†1444) —depict this Thomist truth about the Incarnation. They capture the moment of the Incarnation by painting the embryonic Christ advancing toward the Blessed Virgin, already carrying a miniature cross. For his part, Hans Memling omits this detail in his 1480 oil-on-wood portrayal of the scene. He does however depict the Virgin in a room brightly painted blood red.

At the Annunciation we learn that the Blessed Virgin Mary stands dead center in the struggle that accompanies the history of the human race or, more particularly, in the struggles that mark the salvation histories of each member of the Church. For Mary gives birth to the Son —the "offspring"—who is at "enmity" with the serpent (see Gn 3:15).

In her first joy then, we join Mary in her private chamber, her blood-red room, and rejoice at her conformity to the divine will. Within this red-painted chamber, the Virgin Mary conceives in her womb the Church, the Body of Christ. The private chamber also suggests Mary's virginity. She is depicted in the setting of a virgin, an enclosed place where she remains separated from the bustle of the world. She dwells still within the cloister of her paternal house. Joseph had not yet taken "his wife into his home" (Mt 1:24). The private chamber may further symbolize the visible Church. It circumscribes the place where God's grace enters a fallen world. This grace comes at a price. We rejoice with Mary at the Annunciation. We rejoice with her also on Mount Calvary. There we will join ourselves to her participation in the blood-red sacrifice of the blessed fruit of her womb. To prepare for this holocaust, Jesus says to the Father, "but not what I will but what you will" (Mk 14:36). Mary's joys segue into her sorrows.

At the first joy of Mary, we celebrate a marriage feast. In the mystery of the Incarnation, God establishes an indissoluble bond of grace between Himself and his People. Because she is the first human person to benefit from this bestowal of divine goodness, the first to become a child of the divine predilection, we hail Mary as "full of grace." On Good Friday, we mourn the death of the Bridegroom, who "was pierced for our offenses, crushed for our sin" (Is 53:5). In the mystery of the Passion, God perfects his People whom the red blood of his Son washes clean. At the Annunciation, we salute Mary —in the words Dante places on the lips of St. Bernard—as the "daughter of your Son."[3] On Good Friday, we invoke Mary as the Sorrowful Mother who before all others experiences the meaning of Jesus' words, "My soul is sorrowful even to death" (Mk 14:34). Or as the Psalmist prays, "Here I am, Lord; I come to do your will" (see Ps 40). What an encouraging lesson for the Christian people who invoke Mary in their trials: Mary's joys coexist with her sorrows.

Both the joy of the Annunciation and the sorrow of Good Friday unite us to the mystery that Christ introduces into the world. At the Annunciation, we rejoice to know that God binds himself to our race, such that from the moment of Mary's *Fiat* until the end of time, God's goodness prevails over every form of human iniquity and weakness. On Good Friday, we grieve to discover at what price so abundant a grace is won. How can we reconcile these two emotional responses to our salvation? How can we both rejoice and grieve at the same time? Bl. John Paul II supplies us with the answer: "Before God and before the whole of humanity, Mary remains the unchangeable and inviolable sign of God's election. This election is more powerful than any

experience of evil and sin, than all that 'enmity' which marks human history. In this enmity-marked history, Mary remains a sure sign of hope."[4] No wonder the Church invokes Mary as *Causa nostrae laetitiae*, Cause of Our Joy![5]

The Annunciation beckons us to ponder the theological virtue of faith. We know that the faith of the Church unites all who have hoped for and all who now hope in the Messiah. The unity of the two covenants stands at the heart of the new, graced dispensation that occasions Mary's first joy. The promise of this new grace comes after original sin and finds its first expression known from divine revelation in the faith of Abraham, our father in faith. Mary's first joy then constitutes her as the Fair Daughter of Sion. She stands at the juncture of the two covenants that God established with the human race. About these, St. Paul allegorizes: "These women [Hagar and Sarah] represent two covenants" (Gal 4:24). In Mary, faith and obedience receive a new efficacy. In the first centuries of the Church's existence, the Fathers of the Church delighted to point out the comparison between the disobedience of Eve and the obedience of Mary. The Latin authors observed that the word for Eve, "Eva," backwards spells "Ave."

Spiritual authors point out that Mary's *Fiat*, her assent to the divine plan announced by the angel, inaugurates the new dispensation. In this new dispensation of God's mercy, the 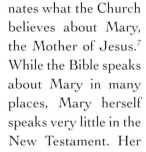 Incarnate Son of God teaches us everything that we need to know, while the Holy Spirit makes it possible for us to observe all that we are taught.[6] This divine gift is called living by faith.

Mary appears everywhere in the Bible. As early as 1977, Pope Benedict XVI recounted the many ways in which the Bible refers to Mary. His book, translated into English as *Daughter Zion*, lists both the citations in the Old Testament that prefigure the Blessed Virgin Mary as well as the New Testament texts that speak of her. Each illuminates what the Church believes about Mary, the Mother of Jesus.[7] While the Bible speaks about Mary in many places, Mary herself speaks very little in the New Testament. Her words however form the basis for an authentic Christian spirituality. *Fiat*. "May it be done to me according to your word" (Lk 1:38b). This justly celebrated word of Mary establishes the primordial form for all Christian existence. We call it the obedience of faith. "Behold, I am the handmaid of the Lord" (Lk 1:38a). Mary's *Fiat* conveys the posture that Christians adopt when they accept themselves as instruments of the divine work in the world. Whether occupying a post of great importance or standing at a humble station, the faithful Christian remains receptive to the influence of God's grace, and so allows God to move him or her according to the infallibly righteous plan of his efficacious will.

Mary's first joy supports the thesis that autonomy fosters an illusion in the human creature. The very fact that God creates each one of us means that each human person radically depends on this creating God. Mary reverses the curse of Eve. The first parents aimed vainly to establish a place of autonomy, a place away from God, and thereby committed the primordial sin of pride. For her part, Mary submits to the divine will and therein finds her vocation and her glory. "May it be done to me according to your word." This submission on the part of Mary establishes her as the model for all Christians. It expresses her humble obedience in faith.

Some versions of Mary's joys include the Visitation. In fact, the longest quote that the New Testament places on Mary's lips appears in the Gospel of Luke, 1:46–55. The words fall within the account of Mary's visit to her elderly and pregnant cousin, Elizabeth. In the exchange between these two women and mothers, we find the prayer that we know as the "Magnificat." Mary gives praise to God for the grace that He has bestowed on her. The grace appears in the form of motherhood.

Psychologists comment on the fact that the original unity between mother and child represents one of the best examples of communion between two persons. No wonder then that the divine pedagogy, God's plan for our salvation, includes this communion between mother and child. From the moment that the angel Gabriel announces to Mary her role in our salvation, maternity takes on a new and supernatural meaning. Because of Mary's divine maternity, there exist two kinds of generation in the world. The generation according to the flesh stands at the origin of human life and accounts for the procession of generations that makes up the history of the world. The other generation comes from the Holy Spirit, who abides as the source of our new and everlasting life.

As Christ himself explains to the Pharisee Nicodemus, "You must be born from above" (see Jn 3:7). Generation according to the Holy Spirit stands at the beginning of the Christian vocation. As the *Catechism* says, "The Father ... determined to call together in a holy Church those who should believe in Christ."[8] At the center of this divine plan stands inseparable from Christ a young and humble maiden, the ever-virgin Mary of Nazareth.

Mary's "Magnificat" expresses her dependence on God. She says that her soul magnifies the Lord, that her very being proclaims the greatness of the Lord. Because she relies on God, Mary's spirit rejoices in God her Savior. No wonder that the Church sees in Mary the icon of the Church in her ultimate perfection. What Mary has received she receives also for us. She fulfills her maternal role in those who remain united with her Son. This extension of the divine maternity confirms Mary's dignity among all women. "Blessed art thou among women!" Throughout the world, the Church venerates Mary as the Fair Daughter of Sion. All that God promises the human race finds its realization in the one who alone remains "tainted nature's solitary boast"—to quote the English poet, Wordsworth.[9] Mary sums up the hymn of praise and glory that should find its place on the lips of every Christian. Just as Mary becomes the Cause of Our Joy, so her "Magnificat" creates the model prayer of every Christian believer.

Notes

[1] *Redemptoris Mater*, no. 11.

[2] See Pope Benedict XVI, Visit to the Cathedral of Cologne, Address of His Holiness Pope Benedict XVI. Cologne, Roncalliplatz, Thursday, 18 August 2005: "...that Thomas Aquinas, the greatest theologian of the West, studied and taught here..."

[3] Dante Alighieri, *Divina Commedia, Paradiso*, Canto 33, 1: Vergine Madre, figlia del tuo figlio, / umile e alta più che creatura, / termine fisso d'etterno consiglio." This usage falls under what is known as "appropriation." Although like all other creatures, Mary is created by God, Father, Son, and Holy Spirit, Christian authors appropriate her creation to the Eternal Son as a "manifestation of the truth" (see *Summa theologiae* I, q. 39, a. 8) that Catholics sing in the familiar Marian hymn attributed to Venantius Fortunatus (c. 530–c. 610) "The God Whom earth, and sea, and sky, / Adore, and laud, and magnify, / Who o'er their threefold fabric reigns, / The virgin's spotless womb contains" (translated from Latin to English by John M. Neale, in *The Hymnal Noted*, 1854).

[4] *Redemptoris Mater*, no. 11.

[5] The Litany of the Blessed Virgin Mary, also known as the Litany of Loreto (Litaniae lauretanae), was originally approved in 1587 by Pope Sixtus V. As early as 1558, however, Catholics used its invocations at the Shrine of Our Lady of Loreto in Italy to implore Mary's intercession. Mozart composed a setting for this popular expression of Catholic devotion: "Litaniae Lauretanae de Beata Maria Virgine."

[6] St. Thomas Aquinas puts it clearly: "Filius ergo tradit nobis doctrinam, cum sit Verbum; sed Spiritus Sanctus doctrinae eius nos capaces facit" (*Lectura in Iohannis evangelium* 14:26; Marietti ed., no. 1958). "Since he is the Word, the Son hands over to us holy teaching, though the Holy Spirit makes us capable of observing his teaching" (author's translation).

[7] See Joseph Ratzinger, *Die Tochter Zion* (Einsiedeln, 1977), English trans., *Daughter Zion*, trans. John M. McDermott (San Francisco, 1983).

[8] *Catechism of the Catholic Church*, no. 759, citing *Lumen gentium*, no. 2.

[9] William Wordsworth (1770–1850), "The Virgin" expresses this thought: "Woman! above all women glorified, / Our tainted nature's solitary boast."

The Nativity
of the Lord

Gaude, sine partu tristi
Virgo partum edidisti
Immo gaudens protulisti
Prolem mater filia

Rejoice: a Virgin: you gave birth,
without painful labor;
nay, you brought forth your Son rejoicing,
you His Mother, His daughter.

he second joy for Mary arrives when she gives birth to the Savior of the world. Christ's birth at Bethlehem reveals an important truth about how God arranges for our eternal salvation. Christians confess that God sent his own Son into our world. This means that the Incarnate Son of God entered as well into our history. The city of Bethlehem still forms part of human history; babies are still born within its borders. So it is natural for us to be curious about the times when Jesus lived and the places where he walked. Christian pilgrimage affords a good witness to the historical realism of our salvation. From earliest times, Christians have wanted to return to the Holy

Land, to visit the places made sacred by the life and death and Resurrection of their Savior. Hans Memling, however, in order to show that the mysteries of Christ belong to every time and place, depicts the Bethlehem scene after the fashion of the Flanders of his day.

Mary's Bethlehem joy captures Christmas worshipers, who respond by singing the hymns and carols that have become part of our common Christian consciousness: *Venite adoremus*! Come all ye faithful. Joyful and triumphant. O come, let us adore Him, Christ the Lord.[1] These strophes and countless others like them interpret the Church's confession of faith. They proclaim that the Child born of Mary in Bethlehem transcends all human expectations. No rational investigation can uncover for us the mystery of Bethlehem. For the Christian believer, this realization causes no concern, because we possess a source of wisdom that exceeds what reason can uncover. God's very own Truth guarantees what we hold in faith. The Nicene Creed sums it up nicely: "For us men and for our salvation he came down from heaven, and by the Holy Spirit was incarnate of the Virgin Mary, and became man."

Mary's second joy involves her perpetual virginity. Historical speculation can at times mislead the Christian believer. A student of the ancient Near East may point out that perpetual virginity would have been unlikely for a young woman of first-century Bethlehem. If grounds for such a contention exist, then believers grasp better the wonder of God's plan for our salvation. There exist many theological arguments that persuade us of the divine wisdom revealed in the Virgin Birth. One concerns every Christian: Mary's first-born Son remains her only Son. This means that the Kingdom of God can welcome every human being. Bloodlines do not count in getting to heaven. The Letter to the Romans makes this clear: "We know that all things work for good for those who love God, who are called according to his purpose. For those he foreknew he also predestined to be conformed to the image of his Son, so that he might be the firstborn among many brothers" (Rom 8:28–29).

The Gospel of Luke attends to the historical character of the birth of Christ. We can determine the period of world history when Mary gave birth to Christ by calculating from the time when St. Luke introduces the figure of John the Baptist, the Precursor of Christ, for the Gospel of Luke (Lk 3:1–3) specifies the time of John the Baptist's public appearance. To be precise, the Evangelist places his reader somewhere around the years A.D. 27 or 28. That is, "In the fifteenth year of the reign of Tiberius Caesar . . ." (Lk 3:1). Whereas the birth of Christ occurs earlier, during the relatively peaceful reign of Caesar Augustus, the world to which

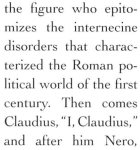

John the Baptist proclaims a baptism of repentance displays the moral chaos that threatens the human race apart from Christ. Tiberius was succeeded by Caligula, the figure who epitomizes the internecine disorders that characterized the Roman political world of the first century. Then comes Claudius, "I, Claudius," and after him Nero, who, mad with grossly immoral dissipation, commits suicide in Rome in A.D. 68. Herod Antipas—that same Herod who put John the Baptist to death—earlier thwarted Nero's proposal to have a statue of his deified self erected in the Temple in Jerusalem. To such a world shaped by urbane Roman imperialism, God sends John the Baptist to prepare the way for the Lord. Urbane Rome with her philosophers and military strategists. Seneca the Younger (3 B.C.– A.D. 65) taught Nero, who later required his tutor to commit suicide for plotting to overthrow him. Into a world characterized by deep personal and social disorders, the Baptist comes to prepare the way of the Lord Jesus Christ. In other words, God knew that urbanity reaches only so far into the human heart. True human happiness requires something more than being urbane or cosmopolitan or bourgeois. Like the shepherds of Bethlehem, we find Him—the something more—"wrapped in swaddling clothes and lying in a manger" (Lk 2:12).

God prepared Mary for the birth of Jesus. Hans Memling shows us the face of a radiant mother kneeling before a newborn who himself rests without the ordinary signs of a child who has just left the womb. We confront the mystery of the Virgin Birth. Mary remains a virgin in giving birth—*virginitas in partu*.[2] This means that the Church holds that Mary gave birth without suffering the pains that giving birth to a child imposes on a woman, and that she suffered no loss of physical integrity. What does God teach us by these miraculous occurrences? The birth of Christ restores the integrity of our human nature, a nature that in one blessed instance finds itself personally united with the second divine Person of the Trinity.

We find this expression of Mary's joy rooted in the grace of the Immaculate Conception.

Mary Immaculate rescues the world from the corruption that would dominate were there nothing to check the spread of human sin. How? God preserves Mary from all stain of mankind's inherited sin. Contrary to what many think, this 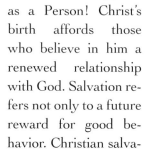 privilege draws Mary close to the rest of the human family. Because of her grace, Mary lives human nature in its perfection. We on the other hand are left to discover what it means to be truly human. This explains why the Jesuit poet Gerard Manley Hopkins compares Mary to "the air we breathe." He wants to proclaim the immediacy that God establishes between the fallen children of Adam and Eve and his Son's Mother. Mary's maternal mediation reveals an important feature of the "logic of the Incarnation."[3] Salvation appears as a Person! Christ's birth affords those who believe in him a renewed relationship with God. Salvation refers not only to a future reward for good behavior. Christian salvation creates here and now a union of persons through which divine grace restores what sinful Adam lost. We become God's adopted sons and daughters, who first discover this deep-down newness in the face of a woman. St. Paul captures the big picture: "When the fulness of time had come, God sent his Son, born of a woman . . . so that we might receive adoption"

(Gal 4:4, 5). To remain alive in Christ, we should invoke Immaculate Mary like breathing out and breathing in. Accordingly, that same poet concludes with a petition: "Be thou then, O thou dear / Mother, my atmosphere."[4]

To become the Mother of our Redeemer, the Virgin of Nazareth was the first to receive from God "every spiritual blessing in the heavens" (Eph 1:3). The saints have never doubted that the Mother of Christ was especially sanctified, even—so St. Thomas Aquinas held—in the womb of her own mother.[5] Now in the dogma of the Immaculate Conception the Church infallibly teaches the precise way that God communicated Mary's unique sanctification:

To her the sin of Adam was not remitted, for she never contracted it. Since she is redeemed, in a more exalted fashion, by reason of the "foreseen merits of her Son," Mary's immaculate holiness prepared her for a great vocation in the Church.[6] For her second joy: the Nativity of the Lord.

What significance does the birth of Jesus hold for the world today? One cannot enter into the mystery of the Nativity without first pondering the text of Genesis that recounts the original deception that led our first parents to recognize their shame. Why does sin necessarily lead to hiding? Some theorists hold that the cause of shame is artificial: had not some moral authority pronounced a deed blameworthy, so they argue, then those who commit such deeds would experience no shame. Catholic doctrine permits no such superficial rationalizations. Because it strikes at the order of life that God has established for his creatures, sin causes shame. To put it differently, every sin constitutes an offense against the dignity of the human person. Sin, to express it still another way, erodes the truth of our being. By their conscious hiding from God, Adam and Eve inaugurate what sinful alienation from God produces in every age: sinners can no longer abide God's presence. The idolatry of the Roman imperial period confirms that even those who have never heard of Christ still hide from God to the extent that they remain loathe to forsake their idols.

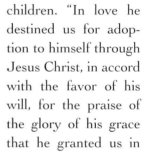

God has established something much better than rationalization and excuse-making for his children. "In love he destined us for adoption to himself through Jesus Christ, in accord with the favor of his will, for the praise of the glory of his grace that he granted us in the beloved" (Eph 1:4–6). Our status as adopted sons and daughters in the One Son ensures that we enjoy the "favor of his will." Those incorporated into Christ become God's "beloved" sons and daughters. As a result, they, that is, we, are destined to remain holy and without blemish, and so to abide full of love. In a word, the birth of Jesus both announces and ensures the universal call to holiness, "that we might exist for the praise of his glory" (Eph 1:12). Reflection on the birth of Jesus again confirms that Mary's joy always becomes our joy. Perhaps this Catholic truth inspired Hans Memling to place two of his contemporaries kneeling in adoration. May we imagine them as representatives of all the baptized?

The second of Mary's joys belongs to her in a special way. There is only one who is the Mother of the Redeemer. In the following excerpt from the Song of Songs (Sg 6:8–10), the Church sees "dove" as allegorically referring to the Blessed Virgin Mary:

There are sixty queens, eighty concubines,
and maidens without number —

One alone is my dove, my perfect one,
her mother's chosen,
the dear one of her parent.
The daughters saw her and declared her fortunate,
the queens and concubines, and they sang her praises;

Who is this that comes forth like the dawn,
as beautiful as the moon, as resplendent as the sun,
as awe-inspiring as bannered troops?

There is only one Immaculate Conception. God provides differently for the rest of us. Our incorporation into Christ, ordinarily effected by Baptism, makes us God's adopted children. Baptism, it is true, frees us from all sin, but it does not remove the disordered concupiscence that gives rise to further sin. And so we are left, as the Council of Trent says, to resist sin by the grace of Jesus Christ. This sort of spiritual combat formed no part of Mary's journey in faith, whereas for us, the baptized, it requires, or should require, a great deal of spiritual energy. When difficult moments arise, Mary, the Mother of Mercy, stays close to her spiritual children. The Catholic tradition reveres Mary as so endued

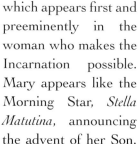

with feelings of compassion that she deserves to be called not only merciful, but even mercy itself.[7]

The birth of Jesus celebrates Christ's complete victory over sin, which appears first and preeminently in the woman who makes the Incarnation possible. Mary appears like the Morning Star, *Stella Matutina*, announcing the advent of her Son. The Immaculate Conception prepared Mary to conceive the Incarnate Word by the power of the Holy Spirit. Her divine espousal left Mary attentive to the voice of the Holy Spirit; her docility makes the Blessed Virgin Mary a woman of hope. This virtue requires receptiveness on the part of the person who must wait for the Lord. And in the Virgin of Nazareth, God has given the world a concrete example of what the Holy Spirit makes out of each of us: an everlasting gift to God's glory (see Eph 1:12). The traditional saying of Catholic spirituality, "Ad Jesum, per Mariam," comes again to mind. To Jesus, through Mary. This adage also expresses the place that Mary wants to occupy in our lives. She deeply desires to direct us to Jesus Christ. With each Christian whom this movement embraces, Mary's maternal mediation achieves a new completion. We find ourselves taken up into the love that never ends, and that, of course, is exactly what every mother wants for her child. Mary gives us Christmas every day of our lives.

Notes

---

[1] The familiar carol "Adeste Fideles" is attributed to the eighteenth-century Catholic layman John Francis Wade, whereas the English version of the text, "O Come All Ye Faithful," comes from the pen of the nineteenth-century Catholic priest Frederick Oakeley. Both were Englishmen.

[2] See *Catechism of the Catholic Church*, no. 449.

[3] Encyclical Letter of Pope John Paul II on the Relationship between Faith and Reason (1998), *Fides et Ratio*, no. 94.

[4] Gerard Manley Hopkins (1844–89), *Poems* (1918), no. 37: "The Blessed Virgin compared to the Air we Breathe."

[5] For the most favorable interpretation of what Aquinas held about the sanctification of the Virgin, see Reginald Garrigou-Lagrange, O.P., *The Mother of the Saviour and Our Interior Life*, trans. Bernard J. Kelly (St. Louis, MO, 1949), pp. 51–71.

[6] Pope Pius IX, Bull, "Ineffabilis Deus" of 8 December 1854: "intuitu meritorum Christi Jesu Salvatoris humani generis" (*Denzinger-Schönmetzer*, ed. 36, no. 2803).

[7] In his *The Secret of Mary* [*Le Secret de Marie*], no. 67, Louis-Marie de Montfort prays that he might practice a continual turning toward Mary's mercy ("un recours continuel à sa miséricorde"). All French texts of quotations from de Montfort are taken from Saint Louis-Marie Grignion de Montfort, *Œuvres Complètes* (Paris, 1966).

THE ADORATION
OF THE MAGI

Gaude, magi procidentes
Tuum natum agnoscentes
Deum regem profitentes
Tria ferunt munia

Rejoice: the Magi prostrating,
recognizing your Son,
professing Him to be their God, their King,
three gifts they bring.

*H*ans Memling placed the Adoration of the Magi at the center of his pictorial narrative of Mary's joys. Among other considerations, his artistic intuition reflects those liturgical sensibilities that rank Epiphany, the feast of the Three Kings, alongside Christmas. The placement also represents the common understanding of the Catholic Church that Christ becomes man to save all men.[1] Epiphany heralds the universality of Christian salvation. As Christmas displays Christ before Jewish shepherds, Epiphany reveals Christ to gentile kings. To this day, the Three Kings remain an irreplaceable feature of Catholic life.

The devotion that the Christian

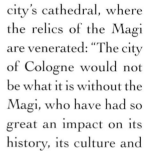

people show toward the Three Kings gives singular expression to the importance of the Epiphany feast. When Pope Benedict XVI traveled to Cologne, he visited the city's cathedral, where the relics of the Magi are venerated: "The city of Cologne would not be what it is without the Magi, who have had so great an impact on its history, its culture and its faith. Here, in some sense, the Church celebrates the Feast of the Epiphany every day of the year! And so . . . I wanted to pause for a few moments of prayer before the reliquary of the three Magi, giving thanks to God for their witness of faith, hope and love."[2] The Magi give witness to the distinctively Christian life that flows from the theological virtues of faith, hope, and charity. Epiphany announces God's plan to make every human being a person who believes divine truth, relies on the divine assistance, and above all, loves with the divine love. No wonder the adoration of the Magi brought Mary her third joy. She recognized before her symbols of God's plan for universal salvation, and beheld, at the same time, something of her participation in this overwhelmingly beneficent divine plan.

Epiphany urges us to embrace life with an assurance of the divine predilection, and at the same time to sustain our conformity to Christ: "For those he foreknew he also predestined to be conformed to the image of his Son, so that he might be the firstborn among many brothers" (Rom 8:29). Some preachers emphasize the responsibility attached to Christian life, and urge Christians to live out their Christian lives keeping ethical obligation first of all in mind. The word "responsibility" however seems an awkward expression to use in the context of God's superabundant, predestining love. Perhaps it is better to say that we should embrace our predestination, which is to remain always conformed to the grace of Mary's Son. Since the virtue of charity comes only as a gift from God, we find ourselves moved under the impulse of this gift in a way that makes ethical duty-keeping appear as a pale counterfeit of the grace that inspires us to lead a holy life. One finds it difficult to praise Our Lady for being "responsible." The invocation "Virgin, Most Responsible" would sound quite odd to the ears of faith. This moral notion proves too thin and partial to capture the grace that God gives to us through the Blessed Virgin Mary. To comment on her responsibility would eclipse something of her superabundant grace. God's

grace so informs Mary's life that her sense of moral obligation gives way to instinctual expressions of divine love. Those who live recollectedly in Mary can experience this same joyous disposition toward the moral life.

Mary rejoices above all in the divine plan that unites in her Son all persons on the face of the earth. The gifts of the Magi display certain

key dimensions of this providential plan. One king brings gold. Gold symbolizes Christ's universal governance, his kingship over the nations. Another brings

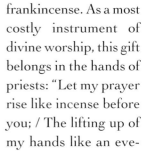

frankincense. As a most costly instrument of divine worship, this gift belongs in the hands of priests: "Let my prayer rise like incense before you; / The lifting up of my hands like an evening sacrifice"—so the Byzantine liturgy sings.[3] Incense symbolizes Christ's perfect worship of the Father. A third king brings myrrh. This substance serves a man who would be buried after death. Myrrh, a perfumed gum resin, forestalls the putrefaction of death. Myrrh symbolizes Christ's death and burial. At the visit of the Magi, Mary discovers that Christ's salvific sufferings and death will cast their shadow even over the joyous events of his life.

Some accounts include the Presentation of the Christ Child in the Temple among the Seven Joys of Mary: "And when the time came for their purification according to the law of Moses, they brought the Child up to Jerusalem to present him to the Lord" (Lk 2:22). The Temple represents a place of consecration. For Christ to save all men requires his passing through the Temple (see Heb 9:11–12). We see how the mysteries of the Infant Christ foretell the mysteries of the Suffering Christ: the circumcision of the Child Jesus; Mary's purification; and the redemption of the first-born male, which the Scriptures connect with purification (see Lk 2:21–24). These biblical mysteries foreshadow the reformation of life that baptismal vows require of those who pronounce them: permanence, purification, and self-offering. The mysteries of the Temple also ground the theological life, which means nothing more than an everyday life lived in faith, strengthened by hope, and informed with charity. These virtues point toward the essentials of Christian life: transformation, forgiveness, and love.

First, the circumcision of the Christ Child: we recognize the permanent character of our baptismal transformation. At the same time, the first shedding of blood points to Christ's ransoming of our souls. Then, "when the days were completed for their purification" (Lk 2:22), Mary and Joseph come with the Child to the Temple. Simeon and Anna receive them. To manifest the divine work at play, the parents of Jesus bring the offering prescribed for the poor, "a pair of turtledoves or two young pigeons" (Lk 2:24). The Presentation inspires confidence in those who do not perceive greatness in themselves. God asks that we give him our whole hearts, whatever their contents, and that we allow him to transform them. So at the Presentation, Louis-Marie de Montfort rhapsodizes: "Hail Mary! I adore your Offering. It is a child. I make him the master of my whole being, inasmuch as he makes himself my bail."[4]

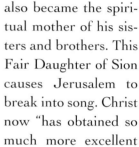

Second, the purification of the Blessed Virgin Mary: we marvel at what Bl. John Paul II calls Mary's "motherhood in the Holy Spirit."[5] When she gave birth to Jesus, Mary also became the spiritual mother of his sisters and brothers. This Fair Daughter of Sion causes Jerusalem to break into song. Christ now "has obtained so much more excellent a ministry as he is mediator of a better covenant, enacted on better promises" (Heb 8:6). To prepare us for the excellence of life that Christ obtains, Mary envelops each of us in her maternal mediation. Purification entails suffering, however. So the aged Simeon prophesies of Mary: "And you yourself a sword will pierce" (Lk 2:35). We specially welcome Mary's maternal mediation during those moments when the purification we must undergo weighs heavily on us.

Third, the redemption of the first-born male: we glimpse the soteriological dimensions of our own Christian vocation. As St. Paul reminds us, "Or are you unaware that we who were baptized into Christ Jesus were baptized into his death?" (Rom 6:3). Those who merit a share in Christ's death, his unique self-offering, should rejoice to make of their lives an offering to God. Like an overture to a great opera, the joys of Mary that surround the adoration of the Magi evoke the sacrifice of her Son. In the stanza devoted to the Presentation, Conrad of Haimbourg captures something of the self-offering required of every Christian: "Rejoice: your Son, whom you nursed, / him you presented in the Temple, / and you, a Virgin, made atonement / with the sacrifice of those giving birth." The Church prays, "May he make of us an eternal offering to you, so that we may obtain an inheritance with your elect, especially with the most blessed Virgin Mary, Mother of God."[6]

In the liturgical calendar, the Baptism of the Lord serves as the octave day for the feast of the Epiphany. If we think back on the feasts of the Christmas cycle, we can easily recognize a common grace. The mysteries of this season communicate the grace of our personal transformation into Godly people. Throughout the Christmas liturgies, we hear again and again a theme that dates from the first centuries of Christianity: "For the Son of God became man so that we might become God." The great defender of Christ's divinity against the Arians, St. Athanasius, receives credit for this formulation.[7] All that brings Mary joy illuminates some aspect of this cardinal tenet of the Christian faith.

A feast day that points to our own baptismal conversion brings to a close the joys associated with the Infant Christ. We find ourselves ready to believe in our own transformation. To hope for its final completion. Above all, to love in a way that reflects our "new nature." Our transformation in Christ. As a very practical gift, Baptism enables us to love with confidence, allowing us to honor each day our baptismal transformation, though we increasingly gain understanding about the place that suffering holds in the life of the Christian. Mary knows that no follower of Christ escapes sharing in her Son's own consecration, a consecration foretold in the Temple and completed on the Cross. Christ himself speaks of his dolorous baptism—his "cup"—to the Sons of Zebedee—young apostles who imagined joy without suffering: "My cup you will indeed drink, but to sit at my right and at my left [, this] is not mine to give but is for those for whom it has been prepared by my Father" (Mt 20:23). Observe that Hans Memling did not fail to include the Slaughter of the Holy Innocents (see Mt 2:16)

in his depiction of Mary's joys. The artist wants to remind us that even amidst her joys, Mary recalled the price of her Son's consecration: his payment, his atonement, which the Presentation in the Temple foreshadows.

During Advent, John the Baptist announces the arrival of Christmastime graces. As the season comes to a close, the Baptist stands on the banks of the River Jordan. His figure reminds us that Christ's Baptism in the Jordan signals the "baptism" of his bloody death (see Mt 10:38). The Baptism of the Lord prepares us for Mary's Easter joys. Happily, the liturgical calendar places an interstice between the joys the Infant Christ brings to Mary and those the Risen Christ affords her.

The Church reserves for us a period of Ordinary Time. There we find the liturgical leisure to savor Mary's joys that flow from her divine maternity. We need this time to let the miracle of our transformation work in us.

The arrival and the departure of the Magi supply the central image of Memling's representation of Mary's Seven Joys. They leave behind gold for a king, whose crown will be of thorns. Frankincense for a priest, who on the Cross will offer himself as Victim. Myrrh for one who will be buried in a garden tomb. The Epiphany both foretells and recapitulates the events of Christ's public life that end on Calvary. On that mountain, Mary earns the titles Mother of Sorrows and Our

Lady of Compassion. Without felt disturbance, the bright dawn of Easter morning returns Mary and us to the joys of the Risen Christ. For "Mary Magdalene, Mary, the mother of James, and Salome bought spices so that they might go and anoint him. Very early when the sun had risen, on the first day of the week, they came to the tomb" (Mk 16:1–2).

To introduce his depiction of Mary's next joy, Hans Memling includes these three holy women on their way to the tomb, while at the same time he illustrates the *"Noli me tangere,"* Christ's response to Mary Magdalene when she recognized him as the Risen Lord: "Stop holding on to me, for I have not yet ascended to the Father" (see Jn 20:11–18, at 17). The Child whom Mary held up before kings and carried into the Temple has completed his earthly work, and a new set of relationships unfolds.

Notes

[1] The translation of the Nicene Creed maintains this linguistic usage to show what the Latin original makes clear, namely, that the human nature that the Eternal Son assumed is one with the common nature of all human beings that Christ came to redeem.

[2] Address of His Holiness Pope Benedict XVI, Visit to the Cathedral of Cologne, Cologne, Roncalliplatz, Thursday, 18 August 2005. The Pope explained the presence of the relics in Cologne: "You should know that in 1164 the relics of the Magi were escorted by the Archbishop of Cologne, Reinald von Dassel, from Milan, across the Alps, all the way to Cologne, where they were received with great jubilation. On their pilgrimage across Europe these relics left visible traces behind them which still live on today, both in place names and in popular devotions. In honour of the Magi the inhabitants of Cologne produced the most exquisite reliquary of the whole Christian world and raised above it an even greater reliquary: Cologne Cathedral. Along with Jerusalem the 'Holy City,' Rome the 'Eternal City,' and Santiago de Compostela in Spain, Cologne, thanks to the Magi, has become down the centuries one of the most important places of pilgrimage in the Christian West."

[3] See "Vespers: The Evening Liturgical Prayers according to the Byzantine Rite Tradition," Byzantine Leaflet Series No. 29 (Pittsburgh, 1983).

[4] Louis-Marie de Montfort, *Cantiques* 90, 15, "Je vous salue, Marie, / Dans la Purification! J'adore votre Hostie, / c'est un poupon. / Je le rends maître / De tout mon être, / Puisqu'il se fait mon caution" (ed. Paris, p. 1353).

[5] *Redemptoris Mater*, no. 44: "Mary is thus present in the mystery of the Church as a model. But the Church's mystery also consists in generating people to a new and immortal life: this is her motherhood in the Holy Spirit. And here Mary is not only the model and figure of the Church; she is much more."

[6] *Roman Missal*, Eucharistic Prayer III: "Ipse nos tibi perficiat munus aeternum, ut cum electis tuis hereditatem consequi valeamus, in primis cum beatissima Virgine Dei Genetrice Maria."

[7] *The Catechism of the Catholic Church*, no. 460, n. 80 cites St. Athanasius, *De incarnatione*, 54.3 (PG 25, 192B).

The Risen Christ's Appearance to His Mother

Gaude, quia tuus natus
In mortem pro nobis datus
Te vidente tumulatus
Surgit cum victoria

Rejoice, for your Son,
delivered to death for us,
buried, you seeing it,
rises in victory.

*M*emling's representation of the Seven Joys of the Virgin illustrates the ancient tradition that the Risen Christ first appeared to his Mother.[1] No less an authority than St. Ignatius of Loyola attests that the Risen Christ first of all appeared to his Mother. Christ appears like the rising Easter sun. Mary

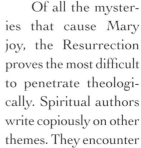

precedes him as the morning star and dawn. Mary's unspeakable joy at the Resurrection of her Son catches on contagiously, and like the Easter fire spreads rapidly throughout the whole Church. *Regina coeli, laetare, alleluia.* The Paschal fire will never die out. It will continue to burn until that moment which "only the Father" (Mk 13:32) knows. Until then,

"The Church believes that Christ, who died and was raised up for all, can through his Spirit offer man the light and the strength to measure up to his supreme destiny."[2]

Of all the mysteries that cause Mary joy, the Resurrection proves the most difficult to penetrate theologically. Spiritual authors write copiously on other themes. They encounter difficulty composing on Easter. Easter falls instead to the pens of hymn writers and poets. Just as philosophers have trouble agreeing on being, so scholars lack agreement on what new being, new life, means. When concepts fail, only prayer remains. So on the night before Easter, the Church asks us to keep vigil and to maintain a prayerful disposition. The Church knows that it takes time for Christians to absorb the meaning of the Paschal mysteries. Discovery of the full dimensions of the new life, the new being that Christ's Resurrection introduces into this world of old being, requires our careful attention to the Word of God.

Christ's Resurrection affects the history of the world, backwards and forwards. "If, then, we have died with Christ, we believe that we shall also live with him" (Rom 6:8). The once-and-for-all sacrifice for our sins has been completed. Everything is changed. The Latin Church Father Tertullian calls Christ the *Illuminator antiquitatum*.[3] The Illuminator of ancient times. Once Christ has broken the chains of death, everything becomes Christian: creation, the garden of Eden, the River Jordan, the Fall, Noah's Flood, the patriarchs Isaac and Abraham, Moses and the Exodus, the prophets, the new Jerusalem, the Last Things. Everything that has gone before and everything in the future become taken up into what the Church calls the "power of this holy night."[4] No other night dispels all evil, washes away guilt, restores lost innocence, brings us peace. Only through the life, death, and Resurrection of Christ do we gain salvation.[5] The Church approves no irenic compromises. No false and misleading inclusiveness. No relativism. She approves only Easter: For this is the night when Christ sheds his peaceful light on all mankind.[6]

Mary is the first to know of the Resurrection of her Son. His expected—we assume—visit brings her joy. In the artist's plan, we see the Risen Christ portrayed in a position similar to that of the archangel Gabriel. Now the Good News announces that God has completed the world's salvation. This announcement causes Mary great joy. Not only joy at seeing her Son again, but joy that arises from deep within the heart of a woman who realizes all that his Resurrection means for the world. In order to grasp something of the joy that seeing her Risen Son brings Mary, we should recall the essential elements of the Easter Vigil. Throughout the Christian world, believers observe Holy Saturday night as a time of special prayer and reflection. We keep company with Mary whose joy already suffuses the liturgical action.

"Then God said, 'Let there be light,' and there was light" (Gn 1:3). During the Easter Vigil, the liturgy turns each Catholic Church into the universe—microcosmically, as it were. Wherever Christians celebrate the Easter Vigil, the same metamorphosis occurs. The fire, which is blessed outside the walls of the church, brings us back to "the beginning, when God created the heavens and the earth" (Gn 1:1). Genesis reveals that no world exists other than the one God made and redeemed: "Thus the heavens and the earth and all their array were completed" (Gn 2:1).

Each participant in the Great Vigil processes behind the blessed flame — the new fire, the Paschal fire — from the open space, the universe of nature, into the body of the church, the universe of grace. There they pray that Christ would shed his peaceful light on all mankind. That Easter grace would envelop the whole of one's city, one's country, one's universe.

A deacon sings the Easter Proclamation. On behalf of all people, the deacon asks, "What good would life have been to us, had Christ not come as our Redeemer?" It raises a question no human being can truly avoid. What good would human life be without knowing Christ? Those who gather around the Paschal candle believe that the answer is simple: No good. No good

at all. Easter heralds the "newness of life" (Rom 6:4) that first appears on "the night when Jesus Christ broke the chains of death and rose triumphant from the grave." Mary watches stilly. All that transpires in the Easter Liturgy, indeed in any Catholic liturgy, makes sense only in light of old Adam's sin. No wonder the *Catechism of the Catholic Church* calls original sin "an essential truth of the faith."[7] Easter, however, allows us to see the "ultimate meaning" of both original sin and our own sins.[8] For us however, this mystery must remain paradoxical: "O happy fault, O necessary sin of Adam, which gained for us so great a Redeemer." No one grasps the truth within this paradox better than Mary.

"So great a Redeemer." The Easter Vigil includes seven readings from the Old Testament. The number seven symbolizes perfection in the things of earth. Just as the Seven Joys of Mary symbolize the perfection of Christian joy on earth, so seven readings capture the message of Moses and the prophets. The seven prescribed Old Testament readings contain prophetic "prefigurations" that now give way to the "ultimate truth of God's revelation."[9] So the faithful congregate under dimmed lights. As St. Augustine explains, "The New Testament lies hidden in the Old and the Old Testament is unveiled in the New."[10] What is unveiled? The true meaning of the Passover. What does Easter celebrate? "Our

Passover feast, when Christ, the true Lamb, is slain, whose blood consecrates the homes of all believers." Mary ponders these mysteries in her heart.

"So great a Redeemer." Let us consider each reading in order. "Christians," we are told, should "read the Old Testament in the light of Christ crucified and risen."[11] Isaac is understood to be a figure of Christ: "Early the next morning Abraham saddled his donkey, and took with him his son Isaac . . . with the wood that he had cut for the holocaust" (see Gn 22:3). Why read about Father Abraham? Because he announces the "obedience of faith" (Rom 1:5) that flows from our baptismal commitment. Why read about Isaac? Because he typifies the innocent Christ who, on the wood of his Cross, offers the perfect holocaust, each day renewed sacramentally in the Eucharist. Moses also prefigures Christ: The escape through the Red Sea remains the central image of the image-rich Paschal liturgy. "But the Israelites had marched on dry land through the midst of the sea, with the water like a wall to their right and to their left" (Ex 14:29). Why read about Moses? Because Easter, O Lord, "is our Passover feast . . . the night when first you saved our fathers . . . and led them dry-shod through the sea." Easter night marks the moment when Christ leads sinful mankind away from the gates of hell. As one early Christian poet sings, "Lo, now to the faithful is opened / The bright road to Paradise leading; / Man again is permitted to enter / The garden he lost to the Serpent."[12] He sings of the Passover of the Lord. Mary rejoices.

"So great a Redeemer." The prophets point to Christ, even as they sustain the expectations of the Chosen People. Why read from the prophet Isaiah? To discover that "wondrous city whose foundations reflect the green and deep blue of the sky and whose golden doors are ablaze reflecting the fire of the sun:"[13] Thus is it written: "I lay your pavements in carnelians, and your foundations in sapphires; I will make your battlement of rubies, your gates of carbuncles, and all your walls of precious stones" (Is 54:11–12). Isaiah makes us yearn for the heavenly Jerusalem. Why read a second time from this prophet? To learn about the nuptial banquet, the paschal banquet, the eschatological banquet: "Heed me, and you shall eat well, you shall delight in rich fare" (Is 55:2). Now Isaiah makes us desire the banquet of divine wisdom. Why read from the "Wisdom Poem" of Baruch? Be-

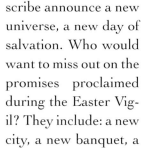

cause this scribe encourages us to prize *phronesis* or prudence, not Aristotle's, but God's own practical wisdom: "Turn, O Jacob, and receive her: walk by her light toward splendor" (Bar 4:2). The splendor of truth, *Veritatis splendor*. And finally, from Ezekiel, who promises that a Godly life springs not from ritual observances but from hearts conformed to Christ himself: "I will sprinkle clean water upon you to cleanse you from all your impurities, and from all your idols I will cleanse you" (Ez 36:25). Together these prophets and a prophet's scribe announce a new universe, a new day of salvation. Who would want to miss out on the promises proclaimed during the Easter Vigil? They include: a new city, a new banquet, a new wisdom, a new heart. The Resurrection of the Christ makes all things new. So we discover the joyful news that no one stands excluded from the goods that these promises contain: "Father, how wonderful your care for us! To ransom a slave you gave away your Son." And this provision of divine wisdom makes Mary rejoice heartily.

Gloria in excelsis Deo. The angels' song at Christ's birth reappears in the liturgy. The lights brighten, the bells sound, the organ plays. And St. Paul exhorts us: "You too must think of yourselves as [being] dead to sin and living for God in Christ Jesus" (Rom 6:11). He is talking about Baptism. Only Christians make bold to address God with words such as these: "By water, made holy by Christ in the Jordan, you made our sinful nature new in the bath that gives rebirth."[14] Then those present at the liturgical ceremony renew as adults the promises that for many were made while they were still infants. The baptized Christian's firm resolve to reject Satan, his works, his promises, flows from the power of Christ's Resurrection. Each person experiences the fulfillment of what was spoken through the prophet Ezekiel: "I will . . . place a new spirit within you and make you live by my statutes, careful to observe my decrees" (see Ez 36:27). Mary's joy overflows.

What happens after the Easter Vigil and the Paschal season? When the parish church shrinks back to its ordinary size. When the Paschal candle is extinguished. When Eastertide gives way once again to the rhythms of Ordinary Time. Where do we find ourselves then? In another kind of microcosm. We call it the human race. Within the human community, living people find themselves at different points with reference to the

Risen Christ. The pagan remains in the darkness; he has not met the light of Christ. Mary urges us to evangelize him. The mortal sinner stands outside the communion of benevolent love; serious sin breaks the bonds of charity that unite man to God. Mary encourages him to repent. The enemy fosters discord; he offends another by his actions. Mary brings harmony and reconciliation. And the friend? Those who abide in the truth? They continue in newness of life. As the poet says, Christ goes on

eastering in them.[15] Among those who remain the friends of Christ, Mary's joy is contagious. Living with Mary helps the Christian to absorb what is inexpressible: the Resurrection of the Lord. All things appear as an expression of the wonderful plan for salvation, even while Mary prays unceasingly that no one pass from this earth outside of God's friendship. Right up to the end, Our Lady of Compassion stands ready to introduce us into the joy of her Son's Resurrection.

Notes

1. *The Spiritual Exercises of St. Ignatius*, trans. A. Mottola (New York, 1964): "He appeared to the Virgin Mary. Although this is not mentioned in Scripture, it is considered as mentioned when the Scripture says that He appeared to many others, for the Scripture supposes that we have understanding as is written "Are you also without understanding?" (p. 122).

2. 1994 Apostolic Letter of Pope John Paul II, *Tertio Millennio Adveniente* on Preparation for the Jubilee of the Year 2000, no. 59.

3. See his *Adversus Marcionem*, Bk. IV, chap. 40 (PL 2:461).

4. The text for the Easter Proclamation may be found in *Roman Missal*, Easter Vigil 18, Exsultet.

5. For further discussion of this Catholic claim, see the Congregation for the Doctrine of the Faith 2000, "Declaration *Dominus Iesus*. On the Unicity and Salvific Universality of Jesus Christ and the Church," no. 13: "In fact, the truth of Jesus Christ, Son of God, Lord and only Saviour, who through the event of his incarnation, death and resurrection has brought the history of salvation to fulfilment, and which has in him its fullness and centre, must be firmly believed as a constant element of the Church's faith."

6. The "Church's commitment to evangelization can never flag. For according to his own promise, the presence of the Lord Jesus in the power of the Holy Spirit will never be absent from her: 'I am with you always, even until the end of the world' (Mt. 28:20)." See Congregation for the Doctrine of the Faith, 2002 "Doctrinal Note on Some Aspects of Evangelization," no. 13.

7. *Catechism of the Catholic Church*, nos. 388–89.

8. *Catechism of the Catholic Church*, no. 388.

9. *Catechism of the Catholic Church*, nos. 128 & 124.

10. *Catechism of the Catholic Church*, no. 129, citing St. Augustine's *Quaestiones in Heptateuchum* 2.73 (PL 34:623).

11. *Catechism of the Catholic Church*, no. 129.

12. *The Poems of Prudentius*, trans. Sister M. Clement Eagan, The Fathers of the Church, vol. 43 (Washington, D.C., 1962), p. 77.

13. Carroll Stuhlmueller, C.P., "Deutero-Isaiah," in *The Jerome Biblical Commentary* (Englewood Cliffs, NJ, 1968) vol. 1, 22:47.

14. *Roman Missal*, Easter Vigil, Blessing of Water.

15. Gerard Manley Hopkins (1844–1889) in "The Wreck of the Deutschland," 35: "Let him easter in us, be a dayspring to the dimness of us, be a crimson-cresseted east, / More brightening her, rare-dear Britain, as his reign rolls, / Pride, rose, prince, hero of us, high-priest, / Our hearts' charity's hearth's fire, our thoughts' chivalry's throng's Lord."

THE ASCENSION
OF THE LORD

Gaude, limbum destruentem
Inde justos eruentem
Christum vides transcendentem
Coelos ex vi propria

Rejoice, seeing Christ destroying Limbo,
delivering from there the just,
transcending the heavens,
by his own power.

"Today Our Lord Jesus Christ ascended into heaven; let our hearts ascend with him."[1] Thus St. Augustine invites us to ponder the fifth of Mary's joys. The Ascension of the Lord marks a new moment in the life of the Church, one characterized by continuity and at the same time discontinuity. Discontinuity, in that Jesus removes himself from our physical vision: "Men of Galilee, why are you standing there looking at the sky?" (Acts 1:11). Continuity, because Christ's return to the Father means that his saving mission goes on: "He ascended on high and took prisoners captive; he gave gifts to men" (Eph 4:8). One and the same feast both commemorates the absence of Christ's human body from the eyes of men and inaugurates his real presence in the Church of faith and sacraments. St. Leo the Great sums up this wonderful orchestration of divine providence, assuring us that, our Redeemer having ascended into heaven, his "visible presence has passed into the sacraments."[2] Mary forms the center of this ecclesial communion that bridges heaven and earth. Her joy reflects the remarkable design of God that makes her Son and Mary herself present to all generations. Hence in her "Magnificat" Mary foretells that "all ages will call me blessed" (Lk 1:48).

The Church shares Mary's blessed joy. Throughout the world, the Church finds cause for great rejoicing on account of Christ's return to his Father. Why? Let Louis-Marie de Montfort suggest a reason that links the Ascension to the sacrament of the Eucharist. In his *Cantique* or Canticle, de Montfort says that Jesus was not able to leave Mary behind on account of the love that bound them. So before his death, Christ established the Eucharist in order that after his Ascension, Mary would find consolation here below.[3] The saints rejoice with Christ. In fact, the saint by definition loves fully what Jesus and Mary love fully.

As Christ's physical body returns to heaven to share completely in the beatitude of his human soul, his Mystical Body on earth learns to anticipate its own heavenly beatitude. The disappearance

of Christ, though a source of initial bewilderment to the Apostles, reveals that God's glory will display itself in you and me. "I will not leave you desolate," Jesus promises, "I will come to you" (Jn 14:18). Indeed, it is only by withdrawing from our physical company that Christ could have made himself personally present to so many different people. We learn this truth about the nature of the Church from St. Augustine, who taught that "although [Christ] ascended alone, we also ascend, . . . because the body as a unity cannot be separated from the head."[4] During the Mass on Ascension Day, the Church prays that each of her members will "follow him [Christ] into the new creation, for his ascension is our glory and our hope."[5] As we ponder in faith the visual representations of Mary's joys, Hans Memling helps us to recognize that this hope finds its first and preeminent realization in the person of the Blessed Virgin Mary.

The artist creates a landscape that his contemporaries would easily recognize as his adopted land. At the same time one espies  another horizon that transcends fifteenth-century Flanders. The careful observer sees that in the painting all creation—mountains, oceans, rivers, hills, flowers and animals—shines with a hue that comes from Mary. The foreground of the painting exhibits the realistic style characteristic of the early Flemish painters. These artists observed closely the details of things and painted them. This native realism marks an important point in the development of Western art, as Christian artists move away from the iconic and symbolic, such as 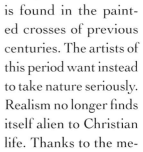 is found in the painted crosses of previous centuries. The artists of this period want instead to take nature seriously. Realism no longer finds itself alien to Christian life. Thanks to the medieval theologians, Catholics came to accept that supernatural grace does not eclipse everyday nature. And so Memling's artistic genius displays for us the truth that divine grace perfects human nature.

St. Thomas Aquinas, whose *Summa theologiae* first gains currency as a theological textbook around the time that Memling composed his painting, provides the theoretical background for this theological breakthrough. At the same time, the artist does not subordinate to an artificial mimesis the sacred mysteries of Christ's life that cause Mary joy. As one moves up the painting, the realism gives way to a more stylized depiction of cities and places: Is the city the painter's adopted Bruges or is it Jerusalem? Are the ocean and ships and mountains in the background realistic depictions of fifteenth-century Flanders, or, as is most likely, pointers to a world beyond? Note that while the ocean horizon stands to the west of what is today Belgium, it seems as if the sun is rising in the east. The whole composition, with elusive miniature figures placed on the mountaintops, announces the mystical

significance of its theme. Like her Son's power that raised Him on high above the heavens, Mary's joy belongs to another world than the one we inhabit. So no need to explain why Hans Memling clearly places Mary on the mountain of the Ascension, although the New Testament makes no explicit mention of her being there in the company of the Apostles.

The fifth of Mary's joys occurs as Jesus leaves us to go to the Father. Shakespeare's "parting is such sweet sorrow" does not capture this joy of Mary. Shakespeare is modern. He plays on irony. Irony arises when transformation fails. There is nothing ironic in Memling's portrayal of the Seven Joys of Mary. His approach does not resemble the Cubism of Pablo Picasso, still less the surrealism of Salvador Dalí. When Jesus ascends above the heavens, his leaving allows room for no expressions of sorrow. Rather, the Ascension completes Mary's joy in a way that is distinctive to the divine plan for our salvation. This moment of completion centers on the destiny of her Son. As for the rest of us, there still remain two more joys to complete our instruction about heavenly glory.

The Ascension brings new empowerment to the Church: "Amen, amen, I say to you, whoever believes in me will do the works that I do, and will do greater ones than these, because I am going to the Father" (Jn 14:12). Since these words find their most effective fulfillment in the seven sacraments of the Church, the words that Christ speaks apply especially to the priests of the Church.

The Ascension illumines their sacramental identity as "other Christs." As the irreplaceable enactors of the Eucharist, they proclaim the mystery of faith, announce the pledge of future glory, and urge us to have charity for one another. These activities form great works that continue in the Church, even though Jesus now reigns gloriously in heaven. "In spite of the withdrawal from our eyes of everything that would command reverence," St. Leo the Great again explains, "Faith does not fail, hope is not shaken, charity does not grow cold."[6] Priests do not exist for themselves. Their lives are consecrated so that the Christian faithful can share in the sacramental provision that, according to Louis-Marie de Montfort, Mary's Son instituted to sustain her joy.

The Catholic tradition associates priests and Mary in a special way. Both serve as mediators of divine grace for the world. Several titles explain the special relationship that the Blessed Virgin Mary, who was not a priest, enjoys with those who are consecrated as priests. The seventeenth-century French school of priestly piety coined the expression "Queen of the Clergy," *Regina Cleri*, while more recently, Bl. John Paul II named her "Mother of Priests." Mary is Queen of the

Clergy inasmuch as she presides over the well-being of the whole Church and the three circles of communion that comprise the recognized vocations. The Church cannot exist without priests. This arrangement does not arise as a result of historical accident. Rather, the Church holds that the place of priests in the Church expresses an ordination of the divine will. No priest serves as an individual agent of his own plans or ideas. By his priestly ordination, a priest enters a specific communion or hierarchy. The clergy include bishops and priests. Mary's title Queen of the Clergy indicates that she rejoices in this provision for the salvation of souls that her Son established on the night before he died.

Mary is Mother of Priests. This title points out another aspect of Mary's relationship to the individual priest. Again, the Church calls her priests "other Christs." For priests act in the name and person of Jesus Christ. As important as the personal holiness of the priest remains to the successful completion of his priestly ministry, God has provided a guarantee more trustworthy than the personal condition of a given man on which to ground the bestowal of divine gifts. The sacramental consecration that priests receive establishes them as effective agents of God's Word and the sacraments. Because they derive this authority and power from the Risen and Ascended Christ, the priests of the Church enjoy a special claim on

Mary's maternity. They remain her sons in a way that surpasses human understanding. Her joy reaches a special peak when the priest faithfully observes the last words that Mary speaks in the New Testament: "Do whatever he tells you" (Jn 2:5).

Christ tells his priests to celebrate the Eucharist for the good of the Church. The blessed Eucharist proclaims the transformative effect of divine power in the world. Here nature and grace reveal their interaction. Grace perfects nature. Our human natures. Our persons. The sacramental action of the priest perfects the humble natures of bread and wine. When this mystery of Transubstantiation occurs, we discover the most real mode of the divine presence among us. In fact, the Church speaks about a Real Presence. For there, in the sacrament of his Body and Blood, we revere Christ present in a most special way (*specialissimo modo*) to his disciples and to the world. The Eucharist inspires religious awe. St. Thomas Aquinas said that wherever priests celebrate the Mass, angels gather together in special configurations. Hans Memling adapts this teaching by placing the angels at the beginning and at the end of Mary's joys. Aquinas also taught that the saints pay uncommon attention to the consecrated species, so much do they grasp how this sacrament unites the Church below with the Church in glory.

The saints disclose the power of Christ's Eucharistic presence. Thérèse of Lisieux, for example, applies the mystery of Christ's physical absence but real presence to our daily lives. She compared herself to a toy—a little ball—which Jesus can pick up and put down as he wills. This metaphor reveals the saint's secret for a holy life. "For some time now," she wrote in her recollections dedicated to her sister, Mother of Agnes of Jesus, "I have offered myself to the Child Jesus to serve as his little toy . . . like a little ball of no value."[7] Like the little host which could not hope to transform itself into the body of Christ, Thérèse looks to no other creature for her spiritual tranquility and peace. It comes as no surprise, then, that Thérèse loved the Eucharist, that she cherished her duties as sacristan at Carmel, that her life of prayer revolved around the most special presence of her Jesus in the sacrament of the altar. Thérèse could make her own the words that disciples at Emmaus used to describe their Eucharistic encounter with the Risen Christ: "Were not our hearts burning [within us] while he spoke to us on the way and opened the scriptures to us?" (Lk 24:32).

As we ponder the completion of Christ's earthly mission, we should make the sentiments of the priest Louis-Marie de Montfort our own. In his devotional guide *Methods for Saying the Rosary*, the saint proposes that at the first bead of the second glorious mystery, the first "Ave" for the Ascension, we contemplate "the promise that Jesus made to his apostles to send them the Holy Spirit and the command that he gave them to prepare for his reception."[8] Mary before all others believes this promise and honors this command. De Montfort points to something of the joy that Mary experiences as she witnesses her Son ascend into heaven.

Notes

¹ St. Augustine, "Sermo de Ascensione Domini" (PLS 2:494).

² St. Leo the Great, "Sermo 2 de Ascensione," (PL 54:397–99), chap. II.

³ Louis-Marie de Montfort, *Cantiques* 134, 1: "Jésus ne peut quitter Marie / Tant l'amour qui les lie est fort, / C'est pourquoi, peu devant sa mort, / Il établit l'Eucharistie, / Pour après son Ascension, / Être ici-bas sa consolation" (ed. Paris, p. 1553).

⁴ St. Augustine, "Sermo de Ascensione Domini" (PLS 2:495).

⁵ *Roman Missal*, The Ascension of the Lord, Opening Prayer.

⁶ St. Leo the Great, "Sermo 2 de Ascensione" (PL 54:397–99), chap. I.

⁷ Thérèse de Liseux. *Oeuvres complètes* (Paris, 1992), "Manuscrit A," p. 177: "Depuis quelque temps je m'étais offerte à l'Enfant Jésus pour être son *petit jouet*, . . . comme d'une petite balle de nulle valeur."

⁸ Louis-Marie de Montfort, *Méthodes pour Dire le Rosaire*, no. 22.1: "Ave; pour honorer la promesse que Jésus-Christ fit à ses apôtres de leur envoyer le St-Esprit et l'ordre qu'il leur donna de se préparer à sa réception" (ed. Paris, p. 415).

THE DESCENT
OF THE HOLY SPIRIT

Gaude, cum in igne misit
Pneuma sacrum, ut promisit
Christus suis, tunc immisit
Tibi hoc in copia

Rejoice, for in fire
Christ sent his [disciples]
the sacred Spirit, as he promised;
it was then [too] he sent you this [Spirit] in plenitude.

To discover why Mary rejoices at Pentecost, we should recall that her divine maternity establishes her in distinctive relationships to each Person of the Blessed Trinity. The faithful daughter of the Father, who became the Mother of the Incarnate Son, is called the Spouse of the Holy Spirit.[1] Pentecost centers on this third

Person of the Blessed Trinity, the one to whose power the Church attributes Mary's conceiving the Eternal Son. Within the Trinity, the Holy Spirit is the person of love, so called because, as St. Thomas Aquinas helpfully remarks, both Father and Son love through him.[2] When the Holy Spirit descends on Mary and the Apostles, we discover that his descent belongs in a distinctive way to those configured to Christ in Baptism. The mission of the Holy Spirit to graced souls introduces them into the life of the Trinity. Recall the hymn that the Church sings whenever she wishes to implore the Holy Spirit. *Veni, Sancte Spiritus: Per te sciamus da Patrem / Noscamus atque Filium.* "Come, Holy Spirit: Through thee may we the Father know, / Through thee the eternal Son."[3] In Memling's painting, a woman contemporary of the artist—in all likelihood the patroness of the arts who commissioned his rendition of the Seven Joys of the Virgin—kneels in prayerful wonder outside of the house where the Apostles and Mary receive the outpouring of grace that comes in the form of wind and fire: "When the time for Pentecost was fulfilled, they were all in one place together. And suddenly there came from the sky a noise like a strong driving wind, and it filled the entire house in which they were" (Acts 2:1–2).

At Pentecost, God invites all who dwell on earth to share in the love that Christ's death makes possible for the human creature. What Epiphany foretells, Pentecost announces. Each human being is called to enjoy a personal relationship with Father, Son, and Holy Spirit. Because of the permanence that God intends for this union, the Church calls the believer's relationship with each Person of the Trinity an "indwelling." The indwelling of the Trinity in the souls of the just expands their knowing and loving to embrace the Father, the Son, and the Holy Spirit. The Church of Christ identifies the place where those marked with the Trinity find their sustenance. This spiritual sustenance chiefly includes the preaching of the Word of God and participation in the Church's sacramental life.

In his depiction of Pentecost, Hans Memling portrays the first priests, the Apostles, in postures that differ from that of Our Lady. The Apostles, who as the first bishops of the Church will initiate the sacramental life of the Church, seem electrified by the outpouring of the Holy Spirit. God inflames these men with a sense of their divinely ordained mission. Their expressions combine wonder and joy. Mary, on the other hand, maintains a serene composure. Her ecstatic joy—symbolized in the artist's conception by her raised hands—occurs at the Annunciation and the Appearance of the Risen Christ. In the sixth joy, we find Mary sitting in the center of the apostolic college with her eyes fixed on the book that she holds on her lap. Her hands folded in

prayer express a contemplative joy. The artist displays something that touches on the complementarities that exist within the Church. The Apostles receive a commission to carry out the work of Christ Head and Shepherd. To them belongs the active part. Mary however, who already possesses everything that her sanctification requires, embodies the contemplative soul. So at

Pentecost, while seated in the middle of the Twelve, Mary gives herself over to the contemplation of the Truth that her Son's Apostles will announce publicly later in the

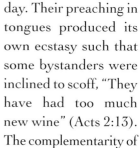

day. Their preaching in tongues produced its own ecstasy such that some bystanders were inclined to scoff, "They have had too much new wine" (Acts 2:13). The complementarity of action and contemplation still informs Catholic life. Those who enter the rhythms of this life experience a spiritual inebriation that comes from the Holy Spirit (see Eph 5:18).

The contemplative vocation that belongs to each Christian finds its most excellent model in the person of Mary. Contemplation brings spiritual joy. The more we embrace the mysteries of God's love for us, the more we find ourselves filled with the joy that worldly pleasure cannot bestow. Since we often think of joy as originating in sense experiences, proper discernment of spiritual joy may require time. The *paideia* of Christian culture plays an important role in helping people discover authentic spiritual joys. Note that Memling's depiction of the Upper Room at Pentecost ranks in dimension with the Adoration of the Magi and the Nativity of the Lord. The artist distinguishes between those mysteries that unfold within a public setting and those that occur in an intimate one. Christmas, Epiphany, and Pentecost invite the participation of others. At Christmas, the shepherds arrive. At Epiphany,

the gentile Magi. At Pentecost, the whole world witnesses the outpouring of the Holy Spirit. This universal audience finds representation in the 3,000 devout folk gathered in Jerusalem from everywhere for the Jewish festival and who were baptized after hearing Peter explain the Christian gospel (see Acts 2:41). By contrast, the Annunciation, the Appearance of the Risen Christ, and the Ascension all partake of a certain intimacy that restricts the presence of persons from the outside. These mysteries involve respectively the angel Gabriel and Mary, the Risen Christ and Mary, the Apostles, somewhat caught off guard, and Mary. Mary best conserves the spiritual joy that the mysteries of Christ, whether public or intimate, announce and create.

Pentecost features another personage. The Apostle Peter occupies a special place before the Blessed Virgin Mary. While the other Apostles stand, Peter kneels. He is the first to recognize the joy that Mary experiences. The same Peter whom the artist faintly depicts walking across  the waters toward the Risen Christ now falls to his knees. The emphasis on Peter reveals the artist's Catholic sensibilities. Peter stands out as the Prince of the Apostles. The Second Vatican Council sets forth clearly what Catholic and divine faith holds about the Petrine office: The Pope, Bishop of Rome and Peter's successor, "is the perpetual and visible source and foundation of the unity both of the bishops and of the whole company of the faithful."[4] No wonder the Church has always defended the freedom of the Church, of the Roman pontiff, and of the bishops. No expectations that arise from prevailing political or social climates can dissuade the Pope from proclaiming the truth of the Church, the *veritas* 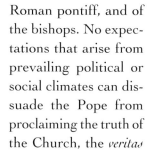 *Ecclesiae*. The Church takes her independence very seriously, and she has done so throughout the centuries-long history of her interaction with lay or secular authorities: "For the Roman Pontiff, by reason of his office as Vicar of Christ, and as pastor of the entire Church, has full, supreme, and universal power over the whole Church, a power which he can always exercise unhindered."[5] The Pope's power ensures that throughout the world the required ministers of the Church will preach the divine indwelling and administer the seven sacraments.

As important as the Petrine office remains for the Church, the saints best illustrate the divine indwelling. Many witnesses present themselves. A special one comes from a French woman who, in 1901, entered the Carmel in Dijon, France, where she received the name Elizabeth of the Trinity. Bl. John Paul II beatified Elizabeth in 1984, and she has become known as the saint of the divine indwelling. We discover something of the instruction that God gave to Elizabeth Catez from this episode that occurred prior to her entrance into contemplative religious life. "In February of 1900, the young aspirant to the Carmel of Dijon was introduced to a Dominican friar, a friend of the nuns. Elizabeth asked for help in understanding her interior experience—her need for silence and recollection, and her sense of an inexplicable presence in the depth of her soul. This Dominican proceeded to deepen her awareness of the truth of the indwelling of the Trinity in the soul of the baptized: that not just Christ, but that 'all three of the Trinity—Father, Son, and Spirit—were present in love in her soul.' This graced meeting greatly reassured Elizabeth and aided her in her spiritual progress."[6] Consecrated contemplative religious, especially women contemplatives, best exhibit the graces of the divine indwelling.

Because of the public nature of the mystery, Pentecost enjoys a representative claim on the sacrament of Confirmation. Those who are confirmed receive "a special outpouring of the Holy Spirit as once granted to the apostles on the day of Pentecost."[7] They discover themselves rooted more deeply in the divine filiation, and so become aware of the Trinitarian nature of their Christian lives. Although the gifts of the Holy Spirit are received first at Baptism, those whom Confirmation unites more firmly to Christ receive an increase of wisdom, understanding, counsel, fortitude, knowledge, piety, and fear of the Lord. At the same time, the presence of the bishop or the use of oil blessed by the local bishop reminds the one confirmed that the Christian life does not flourish outside of a concrete and personal

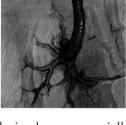

bond with the Church. Within the Church and under the authority of the diocesan bishop, confirmed Catholics express their participation in the joys of Mary by increasing their prayer, especially the "Our Father," and by giving Christian witness.

Like Baptism, Confirmation leaves an indelible spiritual mark on the soul of the one who receives the sacrament. This sign or character expresses the truth that Christ has marked a Christian with the seal of his Spirit. The imprint of the Holy Spirit readies the Christian believer for public witness in marriage or in some special service to the Church. Aquinas speaks about an official commission to evangelize that the confirmed receive in this sacrament.[8] He specifically teaches that Confirmation enables the baptized person "to profess faith in Christ publicly and as it were *quasi ex officio*." *Ex officio* signifies permanent grounds to act in a specific function or "office." The Church takes up this teaching: "Hence [those confirmed] are, as true witnesses of Christ, more strictly obliged to spread and defend the faith by word and deed."[9]

Pentecost grace brings a steadfastness to the Christian vocations that draws its spiritual energy from the joys Mary experienced throughout her earthly life. Laymen and

laywomen glorify Christ as the foundation from which all created reality draws value and meaning. The laity occupy themselves with the sanctification of "temporal affairs."[10] They dwell within the family, the *familiaris consortio*, which the Christian tradition identifies as a domestic church. Their "very special" consecration is marriage, whereas the status of the single person supposes their involvement in ecclesial movements and other forms of dedication.[11]

While consecrated life finds its preeminent expression among contemplative religious like Elizabeth of the Trinity, there also flourish within the Church other forms of ecclesial dedication. In the life of consecrated persons, Christ is contemplated as the eschatological goal to which all tends. The Church teaches that consecrated persons are icons of the Transfigured Christ, who dedicate themselves to him with "undivided heart."[12] Consecrated persons dwell in the circle of fraternal life in communion. This circle includes monastic life; virgins, hermits, and widows; contemplative institutes; apostolic religious; secular institutes; societies of apostolic life; and other, newer forms. Their consecration arises from the profession of the evangelical counsels, of chastity, poverty, and obedience, and as the Church insists, "has an objective superiority."[13]

Mary's Pentecost joy reaches everyone consecrated by Baptism. The divine indwelling comes not as the prerogative of a special few within the Church. The grace that brings our justification flourishes in all those who remain faithful to their baptismal promises. The fact that mere creatures are established as personal lovers of Father, Son, and Holy Spirit leaves the soul without an adequate expression of gratitude. Little wonder that Hans Memling painted Mary with a visage of serene luminosity, a gaze that suggests wonder and praise and high thanksgiving. She knows that within the Church there exist enough graces for all.

Notes

1 For example in *True Devotion*, no. 140, Louis-Marie de Montfort speaks of the reliance on Mary proper to each of the divine Persons.

2 *Summa theologiae* I, q. 37, a. 2.

3 The hymn "Veni, creator Spiritus" is attributed to the ninth-century hymn composer and liturgical theologian Rabanus Maurus.

4 Second Vatican Council, *Dogmatic Constitution on the Church, Lumen gentium,* "Light of Nations," no. 23.

5 *Lumen gentium*, no. 22.

6 Gregory Ross, O.C.D., "Blessed Elizabeth of the Trinity. The Saint of the Divine Indwelling" (privately published pamphlet).

7 *Catechism of the Catholic Church*, no. 1302.

8 See *Summa theologiae* III, q. 72, a. 5, ad 2, cited in *Catechism of the Catholic Church*, no. 1305.

9 *Catechism of the Catholic Church*, no. 1285, and Post-Synodal Apostolic Exhortation of the Holy Father John Paul II Consecrated Life, *Vita Consecrata*, no. 32.

10 *Lumen gentium*, no. 31.2.

11 *Code of Canon Law*, can. 835, ¶ 4.

12 See *Lumen gentium*, no. 42.

13 *Vita Consecrata*, no. 32.

The Assumption
and Coronation of the Virgin

Gaude, Christus cum levavit
Te in carne et locavit
Supra astra, obviavit
Tota coeli curia

Rejoice: when Christ raised you in the flesh,
and placed you above the stars,
the entire court of heaven
went forth to meet you.

he seventh joy of Mary embraces three moments that point us toward Mary's present state of glory. Hans Memling includes each of them in his portrayal of Mary's Seven Joys. These moments include her Dormition, her Assumption, and her crowning in heaven as Queen of angels and saints. As the poem that has provided inspiration for each of the seven of Mary's joys reminds us, these joys surpass the categories of public or intimate. "The entire court of heaven" went forth to meet the Woman adorned with the stars. The Book of Revelation describes her eschatological appearance: "A great sign appeared in the sky, a woman clothed with the sun, with the moon under her feet, and on her head a crown of twelve stars" (Rv 12:1).

Mary's joys reach deep down to the places where original sin introduces sadness into the rhythms of human life. The starting point at once symbolic and real of this inherited sadness occurs at childbirth. Women bring forth children as they endure the pains and danger of labor. Mary's virginity in bringing forth Christ, her *virginitas in partu*, restores gladness to welcoming a child. Although the pains of labor remain as an effect of original sin, Christian mothers rejoice when they see the light of eternal life dawn on their children at Baptism. The endpoint of original sin and the punishments that it visits on the human race arrives at death.

St. Paul makes this point clear in his Letter to the Romans: "just as through one person sin entered the world, and through sin, death, and thus death came to all, inasmuch as all sinned" (Rom 5:12). Adam's sin introduces disorder and death. Death brings its own labor. Its own pains. The pangs of death. The death rattle. The agony. Saints on their death beds have preferred to avoid analgesia. Pope Pius XII counseled that Catholics should await death with as much consciousness as possible, in order to sanctify their last moments on earth.[1]

Christian theologians differ in their views of how Mary completes her earthly journey. Some point to the grace of her Immaculate Conception and her virginal bringing forth of Christ, and so they argue that death took no hold of the woman who was preserved from original sin and its effects. On this first account, Mary's earthly journey did not end in death. Such a point of view represents a consistent application of the place that Mary holds in the plan of salvation. The Mother of the Living herself escapes the sad sentence of death. In the divine plan, then, we draw life from her.

There are other theologians who allow that Mary dies, but peacefully and with a joyous serenity. Eastern Christians, who often speak of her death as a "falling asleep," explain the reason for Mary's serene joy when they proclaim on the feast of the Dormition:

"The grave and death did not detain the Mother of God: she prays perpetually and is our unfailing hope of intercession; for He who dwelt in the womb of the ever-virgin transferred to life the Mother of Life."[2] Whichever opinion one holds, the whole catholic communion agrees that Mary's body did not suffer the corruption of the grave but was assumed by God into heaven.

In his presentation of Mary's deathbed scene, our artist seems to favor the understanding that Mary did undergo death. Memling depicts Mary receiving the Church's ministrations for the dying, while she lies still on her bed. No coffin or bier appears. Note that the Apostles enact the full liturgical action as prescribed

in the fifteenth century. St. Peter, dressed in priestly vestments, leads the last rites for the dying. When the moment came for Mary to depart this earthly life, she still experienced joy. A close look reveals that our artist gives Mary the same placid mien as she reposes on her final earthly resting place that he gives her at the Nativity. After her death, Mary passes over to new life.

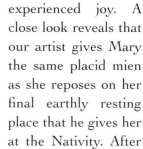

Mary's experience, of escaping the sufferings of death, differs from the human experience of her Son. Because the mystery of salvation that he introduces into the world completely envelops her, Mary remains the first to attain the reward that awaits all those who believe in Christ. We celebrate this joy of Mary under the title of her Assumption. Unlike Christ, who ascends on his own power, Mary is taken up into heaven. The Church has long cherished the belief that the Blessed Virgin Mary immediately enjoyed the crowning moment of Christian salvation. She anticipates the final resolution of things when God makes all things new in Christ. Although the Church defined the dogma only in the twentieth century, the theological reality of the Assumption has dominated Christian culture since the time that early Christian writers pondered the place that Mary holds in Christian salvation. Her glorified body alongside that of Christ's own glorified body gives a dimension to heaven that the angels, sheerly immaterial beings, cannot supply. When we think of heaven as a place, all that we can really imagine is the place where Jesus and Mary stand together. Otherwise, "place" makes no sense when speaking about a God who transcends the limitations of space and time. And Christ does promise us a place: "Do not let your hearts be troubled. You have faith in God; have faith also in me. In my Father's house there are many dwelling places. If there were not, would I have told you that I am going to prepare a place for you?" (Jn 14:1–2).

The Assumption of the Blessed Virgin Mary entails practical implications for Christian believers. Were Mary not raised up body and soul into heaven, her maternal mediation would suffer diminishment through the separation of her soul from her body. She would exist in the same way other saints do, that is, without their bodies. Were Mary not body and soul in heaven, devotion to her would lose its preeminence within the Church. The actual practice of the Church encourages us to remain intimately united with the Virgin Mary, whose ever-blessed person exists, completely, in heaven.

When Christian believers invoke Mary often, when they hail her frequently, they find themselves transported, in a certain sense, to the place where Mary lives with her Risen and Exalted Son. One finds it difficult to imagine a flourishing Marian piety without the prayer that we call the "Hail Mary." Devotion to the Holy Name of Mary affords the most economical recourse to our Blessed Lady. Because of Mary's place within the Church, the Church's practice requires us to revere her in a way that distinguishes devotion to Mary from that directed to the other saints. The saints, apostles, martyrs, pastors, doctors, virgins, holy men and women, receive *dulia*, whereas the Queen Assumed into Heaven receives the high service of *hyperdulia*, which expresses the maximum praise, respect, and service that the Church renders to a creature.

The third moment in Mary's removal from this earth to her place above the skies transpires before the Throne of God. Hans Memling follows a conventional theme when he ascribes to the Exalted Christ the crowning of his Mother. Christ stands ready to welcome his Mother not with an embrace but with a crown. Christ appears as the universal king of the ages, symbolized by his wearing a tiara. Popes once wore this headdress to symbolize their universal jurisdiction over the Church and the sovereignty that the Church enjoys among secular rulers. Mary's Queenship completes her joys. She participates in the governance that her Son has won the right to exercise, by reason of his death on the Cross. Since the event on Calvary, human history has been able to expect no other completion than the judgment that

Christ the King will pronounce at the end of time. Even now, Mary stands at his right hand arrayed in gold (see Ps 45:10). Those who piously and accurately consider the moment of their particular judgment take great comfort from knowing that Mary will stand close to them on a day that Christian sensibility has pictured as one of dread.[3]

How does Mary's maternal mediation affect us at the moment before the verdict of the Last Judgment is uttered (Mt 25:31–46)? Mary stands there as the Refuge of Sinners. All persons inescapably remain subject to the rule of divine justice that the King of Glory will administer as a final judgment on the world. Catholics invoke Mary now and at the hour of their death. For the Christian believer, these two moments form the only ones that really matter. Mary accordingly enjoys a special relationship to the sacraments of healing. Reconciliation or Penance and Holy Anointing bring the poor banished children of Eve special helps for both the present moment and the moment of death. The piety of the Church does not direct us to implore Mary to pray for saints. When we implore Mary "to pray for us sinners," we acknowledge with the Church that even the just person falls seven times a day. Making good and frequent confessions offers the ordinary means for obtaining forgiveness of our sins. At the confessional, Mary remembers us.

When we express sorrow for our sins, Mary rejoices. The Church further warns against falling into the state of final impenitence. This means that one dies without expressing sorrow for sins committed during life. No Catholic should defer the special sacrament for the dying, Holy Anointing. The Church instructs us to call the priest when the time of death or a serious illness that is likely to cause death approaches. This instruction is found in the New Testament: "Is anyone among you sick? He should summon the presbyters of the church, and they should pray over him and anoint (him) with oil in the name of the Lord, and the prayer of faith will save the sick person, and the Lord will raise him up" (Jas 5:14–15).

The Coronation of the Blessed Virgin provides the Christian believer with his or her point of entry to Mary's grace. Each of us takes consolation from recalling the events in Christ's life that bring Mary joy. The Coronation indicates the spiritual place where the faithful actually meet Mary. They meet her today. In the crowned Virgin, living body and soul with Christ, the Church recognizes the spiritual mother of all believers. Each vocation in the Church—clergy, consecrated persons, and lay persons—invokes Mary as its Queen. All the saints—apostles, martyrs, virgins, widows, and so forth—hail Mary as their Queen. Franciscans, Dominicans, Carmelites, Jesuits, and other religious institutes claim Mary as their Queen. Nations make Mary their Queen.[4] The Church acknowledges Mary as Queen of the Universe. No limits fall on her heavenly queenship. Mary receives all with an inclusive love. Before the Queen of Heaven, all find a mother's welcome.

Mary's mediation for the Church reaches universal dimensions. She is that "great sign [which] appeared in heaven: a woman clothed with the sun, the moon beneath her feet, and a crown of twelve stars on her head."[5] The saints have made much of Mary's "maternal role of mediatrix of mercy at [Christ's] final coming."[6] To stress the point, some holy men have opined that Mary's clemency tempers the just wrath of her Son. The intuition remains sound, even if the expression approaches a certain awkwardness. Mary of course provides dying sinners with a place of refuge whence they can invoke the divine mercy. Under her blue mantle, all find the sure comfort that the Mother of Mercy bestows.

When we beg Mary to "pray for us sinners now and at the hour of our death," we prepare to receive the fulfillment of Mary's joy. In heaven, the Seven Joys of Mary surrender to the sole joy that heaven contains: the overflowing happiness that results from seeing God face to face.

Notes

¹ See his "Allocution to Doctors on the Moral Problems of Analgesia," February 24, 1957.

² Kontakion for the Feast of the Dormition (Assumption) of Our Lady, from the *Byzantine Book of Prayer* (Pittsburgh: Byzantine Seminary Press, 1995), p. 586.

³ Perhaps the best-known examples remain Michangelo's *The Last Judgement* in the Sistine Chapel and the hymn known by its opening words: "Dies iræ! dies illa / Solvet sæclum in favilla: / Teste David cum Sibylla!" English translation: "The day of wrath, that day / Will dissolve the world in ashes / As foretold by David and the sibyl!"

⁴ In his Angelus address of 22 August 2010, Pope Benedict XVI observed: "In the history of the cities and peoples evangelized by the Christian message there are innumerable witnesses of public veneration, in some cases even institutional, of the Virgin Mary's royalty."

⁵ *Roman Missal*, The Assumption of the Blessed Virgin Mary, Entrance Antiphon.

⁶ See *Redemptoris mater*, no. 41, with its reference to a homily preached by Saint Bernard: *In Dominica infra oct. Assumptionis Sermo*, 1-2: S. Bernardi Opera, V (1968), 262f.

CONCLUSION

Ecce tibi congaudemus
O Maria, ut amemus
Te in aevum et laudemus
Duc nos ad coelestia

Behold, we rejoice with you, O Mary,
that we may love you
and praise you unto eternity;
lead us to the things of heaven.

The poet whose hymn we have followed, Conrad of Haimbourg, captures the eschatological dimensions of Mary's grace within the Church. Our Carthusian hermit completes his verses on Mary's joy by pleading for the mercy that the Mother of God reserves for those who sin most often. Significantly, however, he envisages that these sinful Christians still call upon Mary's sweet Name and invoke her maternal help and protection. As the Little Flower likes to observe, Mary stands out more as mother than queen. Of course, Mary enjoys both titles. Her maternal mediation extends to the whole world over which she reigns as heavenly Queen. The pastoral implications of the Joys of Mary receive extended commentary in the final strophes of the hymn that accompanies this presentation of Mary's Seven Joys.

Rejoice, O Virgin unrivaled,
that you are exalted before all things;
thus also are you fittingly praised,
O holy one, in celestial glory.

Rejoice, O Virgin, who in your beauty
adorn heaven with the quality of your light,
even as the sun surpasses
all luminaries in splendor.

Rejoice, at whose service as Queen
are the choirs of angels and saints,
and to whom they offer the homage
of their prayers.

Rejoice: whatever you will to regard
appears pleasing to your Son,
and your every supplication
he fulfills with clemency.

Rejoice: those who venerate you
take delight in your praise;
they are rewarded by Christ
in their celestial homeland.

Rejoice: highly crowned,
adorned with the endowments of beauty;
close by the right hand of Christ,
you reign over all.

Rejoice: you shall forever enjoy fully
these genuine delights,
that you may be joyful unto eternity
with the utmost bliss.

Pluck from me now
the joys of this world, mingled with gall;
rather, satiate me
with the honey of your joys.

Come, O Virgin, allow me
to rejoice in you,
to be consoled now,
and at the end to exult in your presence.

Grant me to see you,
to rejoice with you forever,
to possess with you fully
the rewards of the blessed.

Behold, we rejoice with you, O Mary,
that we may love you
and praise you unto eternity;
lead us to the things of heaven.

To sum up the devotion that the Seven Joys of Mary should excite within our hearts, one need only repeat the final words of the hymn composed to celebrate these joys: "Lead us to the things of heaven." Why does this short phrase capture all that is practical, so to speak, about devotion to the Blessed Virgin Mary? The answer comes easily to those who pause to reflect about their lives, who give some time to examining their consciences, who know the difference between virtue and vice, good and bad, holy and sinful. The alternative to sharing Mary's joy in heaven can but make one shudder. Louis-Marie de Montfort describes it this way: "To suffer forever, without merit, without mercy, and without end."[1]

Notes

---

[1] Louis-Marie de Montfort, *Lettre Circulaire aux Amis de la Croix*, no. 21: "A jamais souffir, sans mérite, sans miséricorde et sans fin!" (ed. Paris, p. 234).

www.magnificat.com